THE AHMADAN OUTPOURING
ON THE MUHAMMADAN BIRTH

The Ahmadan Outpouring on the Muhammadan Birth

&

The Song of the New Spring

Tahni'atu 'r-Rabi'

SHAYKH AL-ISLAM & GHAWTH AL-ANAM

Mawlana Abu Ishaq Ibrahim b. Abdullahi Niasse al-Kawlakhi al-Tijani

May Allah be pleased with him and with us on his behalf. *Amin!*

English Translation by
TALUT B. SULAIMAN DAWOOD AL-TIJANI

Edited by
IBRAHIM AHMED DIMSON

First published in 2019 by Fayda Books
2690 Campbellton Rd.
Atlanta, Georgia 30311

www.faydabooks.com
Email: info@faydabooks.com

© Copyright Fayda Books 2019
ISBN 978-1-7339631-2-1

English translation by Talut b. Sulaiman Dawood al-Tijani
Edited by Ibrahim Dimson

No part of this book may be reproduced
In any form without prior permission of the publisher. All rights reserved.

Cover design by
Muhammadan Press

Tyesetting by
Etherea Design

Printed and bound in the United States of America

Contents

Publisher's Foreword
1

The Ahmadan Outpouring on the Muhammadan Birth
7

The Song of the New Spring
23

Poems on the Prophetic Birth
27

Poems in Praise of the Messenger of Allah ﷺ
45

Transliteration of the Poem
57

Translation of the Poem
65

Publisher's Foreword

All Praise belongs to Allah alone! And may the most complete blessings of peace be upon the One whom no prophet or messenger shall follow.

We decided to publish the two beautiful works as one book, with the hopes that it will serve as a source for all who wish to drown themselves in the love of the Prophet, by learning about his reality and praising him with the poetic anthology that is recited annually by Shaykh Ibrahim Niasse ﷺ — our spiritual connection to Allah, the Lordly Pole, the Enduring Aid to the students of at-Tijani, the Possessor of the Divine Flood. The Fayd Ahmadi book is a short work that the Shaykh wrote for the purpose of removing the veil from the eyes of the world regarding the Prophet's origins and how the rest of creation emanates from his light. The Shaykh provides Hadith and historical narratives from the companions of the Prophet, to shed light on this point. He also uses sources like Ibn Ishaqs biography of the Prophet to tell us about the conception, carrying and birth of the Holy Messenger of Allah, by his noble mother and father, Sayd Abdullahi and Sayda Amina (may Allah show His Mercy).

We then followed with the Tahni'a poem, which Shaykh Ibrahim would begin reciting publicly in the Mosque, from the first sighting of the moon of the Prophet's lunar calendar month of Rabi al-Awwal during its nights, after Wadhifa (the daily office), leading up to and including the day of the Noble Mawlid celebration. It had been practiced the same way by the

Mauritanian Shareef, our master, Baddi al-Alawi ﷺ. This poem is part compilation and part original composition of Shaykh Baddi ﷺ. Shaykh Baddi's compilation consists of samples from poetry written in praise of the Prophet ﷺ, from the following poets:

- Abbas, the uncle of the Prophet
- Lisan ad-Deen ibn al-Khateeb, born in Granada, and died in Fes
- Hassan ibn Thabit, the panegyrist of the Prophet
- Ka'b ibn Zuhair, the author of the original "Burdah," or Baanat Su'ad
- Abu Talib (May Allah show His mercy), the uncle of the Prophet
- Imam Busairi, the author of the most well-known "Burdah" or Poem of the Mantle
- And, finally, the composition of Shaykh Baddi himself, sung with the chorus that begins with "*Tahniatur-Rabi'i, Bi Mad-hatish-Shafi'i….*"

Shaykh Baddi himself is a disciple of Shaykh Muhammad Hafiz ﷺ, who in turn was a direct disciple of Shaykh Ahmad at-Tijani ﷺ. His Shaykh, Muhammad Hafiz, brought the Tariqa from Morocco to West Africa proper, by way of Burayna, in Mauritania. It spread from there to Senegal, Nigeria, Niger, Sudan, The Gambia, Ghana, Mali, and so on. Shaykh Muhammad Hafiz, returning from Hajj, went through Fez, met the Shaykh, received initiation and authorization, and was charged to keep his authorization secret until such time that Allah would choose to reveal him to the public. Upon returning to Burayna, someone approached him, requesting from him "the special thing he brought back from his journey…" and by that same night the Tariqa entered every tent in Burayna.

Abbas bin Abdul Muttalib once said to the Prophet ﷺ, while returning from the expedition of Tabuk: "O Messenger of Allah,

I wish to praise you." The Prophet replied: "Go ahead -- nay, may Allah adorn your mouth with silver!" And it is well-known that not a single tooth of his uncle's ever decayed or fell out, until he passed away. He then recited, concerning the Prophet's birth:

> Before it (your descent) you were blessed in the shadows,
> and in the repository, whereof they sought to conceal with leaves
>
> Then you descended to Earth, not yet a human being
> Nor a piece of flesh, neither a clot
>
> But as a pure, seminal drop, you boarded the ark
> When the flood obliterated nasr and its fellow idols
>
> You staved off the fire from al-Khalil while concealed
> Roaming within freely, and were not scorched in the least
>
> Progressing from the purest loins to the purest wombs
> As the world successively appeared in stages
>
> Until al-Muhaymin (The Preserver) made your immense honor issue forth
> from the highest of Khindif[1]
>
> And then, when you were born, a light rose over the Earth, until it illuminated the horizon with its radiance—
>
> And we are now still in that illumination, that original light,
> those paths of guidance—and thanks to them, penetrate and traverse through (the darkness)

Then Shaykh Baddi ﷺ inserts a supplication, so say Ameen afterwards:

---

1   A group of allied and related tribes, of which Quraysh was amongst

> O Allah! We are asking you, by virtue of the one who is being Praised by You and the One Praising, to enlarge and widen our share from that Radiance and Light,

and by it also, guide us to the most right path. Ameen!
And the poet Lisan ad-Deen al-Khateeb ﷺ said in verse:

> O you, who were the Chosen One before even Adam was fashioned (into clay),
>> and before the cosmos even burst forth from its closed state
>
> Is it, then, that the creation purports itself to attempt in praising you,
>> after your character has been praised by the Creator Himself?

Then Salatul-Fatih is recited here. Afterwards, the poetry of Hassan bin Thabit ﷺ is quoted,

> Whenever (while on a nightly stroll) his forehead emerged in pitch-black darkness
>> It would shine like the blazing luminary of dark night.
>
> Who on earth ever was or will ever be the like of Ahmad
>> Either in complete, harmonious conformity with the Truth, or as a warning example to the heretical renegades?
>
> Uniquely emblazoned with the Signet-Seal of Prophethood
>> from Allah, a proof made apparent, and confirmed with eye-witness testimony
>
> And the Lord has drawn together the name of His Prophet to His
>> whenever the Muezzin, crying out the Five, begins saying Ash-hadu (I bear witness!)

And He has extracted it (the prophet's Name) from His name, to have his greatness magnified

> Thus, the Owner of the throne is Mahmood (worthy of all praise), and this beloved one is Muhammad (one who is oft praised)!

Ibrahim Ahmed Dimson
PUBLISHER FAYDA BOOKS

The Ahmadan Outpouring on the Muhammadan Birth

SHAYKH AL-ISLAM & GHAWTH AL-ANAM

Mawlana Abu Ishaq Ibrahim b. Abdullahi
Niasse al-Kawlakhi al-Tijani

May Allah ﷻ be pleased with him
and with us on his behalf. *Amin!*

In the Name of Allah, the Beneficent, the Merciful
May Allah bless our Noble Prophet (SAW)

Ibrahim, the son of al-Hajj Abdullah (who is ever thirsty for the beauty of his Lord) says:

This is "The Ahmadan Outpouring on the Muhammadan Birth." All praise is for Allah with the tongue of the degree that joins between the Names, Attributes, Stations, States, Manifestations and Perfections, who Allah brought into being before the existence of the creation, from the essence of absolute being, who He made him the source of their essences and the reason for their being, who was a Prophet while Adam was between water and clay- nay he was a Prophet while there was no Adam, no water and no clay. I praise him and thank him. And I bear witness that there is no god but He, the First, the Singular who begets not and is not begotten, and there is nothing whatsoever like Him. And I bear witness that our Master Muhammad ﷺ is His slave and Messenger. O, Allah! bless our Master Muhammad, the Opener of what was closed, the Seal of what went before, the Helper of the Truth by the Truth and the Guide to Your Straight Path, and his family in accordance with his grandeur and immense worth.

As to what follows:

Since, Allah, the True King, willed that the light of the Master of Creation should emerge and the He should make it a distinct creation and a separate essence, and to cause, by him, the creation to come to be, out of His sheer grace, generosity and magnanimity, He created our Master Muhammad before creating the veils, the Throne and all that they contain. And He made him a pillar of light, glorifying Allah ﷻ two hundred thousand years before the Throne and the Footstool.

It has been narrated that 'Ali b. Abi Talib (may Allah ennoble his countenance) said:

> Allah created the light of Muhammad ﷺ before creating the Heavens, the Earth, the Throne, the Footstool, the Veils, Paradise, the Fire, the world, the Hereafter, Adam, Shith, Nuh, Ibrahim, Sulaiman, Musa, and 'Isa by seven hundred twenty-four thousand years. After creating him, He created twelve veils. The first veil is the veil of power. The second veil is the veil of greatness. The third veil is the veil of blessing. The fourth veil is the veil of mercy. The fifth veil is the veil of felicity. The sixth veil is the veil of nobility. The seventh veil is the veil of authority. The eighth veil is the veil of guidance. The ninth veil is the veil of Prophecy. The tenth veil is the veil of ascension. The eleventh veil is the veil of obedience. And the twelfth veil is the veil of intercession.

Then, He erected him in the veil of power for twelve thousand years. The whole time the Prophet ﷺ was saying, "Blessed is my Lord, the Most High". Next, He erected him in the veil of greatness for eleven thousand years, where he continuously said, "Blessed is the Knower of that which is secret and that which is more hidden." Then, He erected him in the veil of blessing for ten thousand years, while he was continuously saying, "Blessed is the Most High and Elevated." Then, He erected him in the veil of mercy for nine thousand years, while he was continuously saying, "Blessed is He who is eternal and everlasting." Then, he erected him in the veil of nobility for seven thousand years, while he was continuously saying, "Blessed is the All-Knowing, the All-Wise." Then, He erected him in the veil of authority for six thousand years, while he was continuously saying, "Blessed is the Possessor of the Highest Dominion." Then, He erected him in the veil of Prophecy for four thousand years, while he was continuously saying, "Blessed is Allah and may He be praised. Blessed is Allah, the Immensely Great". Then, He erected him in the veil of elevation for three thousand years, while he was continuously saying, "Blessed is the Holy King." Then, He erected him in the veil of obedience for two thousand years, while he was continuously saying, "Blessed is the Beginningless and Endless." Then, He erected him in the veil of intercession, while he was continuously saying, "Blessed is the King who is worthy of worship."

His uncle, al-'Abbas b. 'Abd al-Muttalib ؓ said:

> Before it you delighted in the shade and in
> A place where the leaves are sewn together,
>
> Then, you descended to the lands, not a man,
> Were you, nor piece of flesh nor a clot,
>
> In purity you boarded the ark, Nasr having,
> Been restrained and his people drowned,
>
> You entered the fire with the Khalil, hidden,
> Being turned about in it, yet you were not burned,
>
> You were transferred from loins to womb,
> When one world passed away, another appeared,
>
> Until your evident nobility rose above,
> Khindif as a high mountain towering over smaller ones,
>
> And when you were born, the earth was,

Split and the horizons were lit with your light,

And we are in that illumination and light,
Being transported to the path of guidance.

Another set of couplets:

O, you who were chosen before the creation of Adam,
While the locks of being had not yet been opened,

Does any created being think they can praise you, after,
The Creator had praised your noble character?

I say, in praise of him ﷺ:

Let mouths forever utter your praises,
O, best of those about whom joy has been expressed,

O, you who are elect among creation before it came to be,
You who are unique having no similitudes,

How could anyone equal him or be his like,
When Allah had decreed his exaltedness in sempiternity,

He is the Intimate Friend [Khalil], the Interlocutor [Kalim] and the Spirit [Ruh],
Perpetually holy because of the matchlessness of his exaltedness,

He is the bearer of glad tidings, the warner and the spirt,
Of this universe. How exalted is he. How beautiful is he,

He is the succor. He is very noble. His existence,
Is the rectification of this universe, so he is its wealth,

Thus, the guidance of Mustafa is the treasure of mankind,
A full moon if you turn towards him, a lion if

You oppose him, an ocean that floods his assembly,

O, Allah! Bless our Master Muhammad, the Opener of what was closed, the Seal of what came before, the Helper of the Truth by the Truth and the Guide to Your Straight Path and his family in accordance with his grandeur and immense worth.

It has been narrated that he ﷺ said, "*The first thing that Allah ﷻ created is my light. And from my light, Allah created all things.*"

It has also been narrated that 'Umar ؓ said that our Master, the Messenger of Allah ﷺ said, addressing him:

"O, 'Umar! Do you know who I am? I am the one whose light Allah created before anything. And that light prostrated to Allah, remaining in that prostration for seven hundred years. Thus, the first thing that prostrated to Allah was my light. And that is no boast. O, 'Umar! Do you know who I am? I am the one from whose light Allah ﷻ created the Throne, the Footstool, the Tablet, the Pen, the light of sight, the light of the intellect that is at the head of all creation and the light of gnosis that is in the hearts of the believers. And that is no boast. O, 'Umar! Do you know who I am? I am the one for whose sake Allah took a pact with the Prophets, Messengers and nations, to confirm my Prophethood and help me, century after century. Allah ﷻ said, *And when Allah took a pact from the Prophets, "Whereas I have given you the Book and the Wisdom, if there should come to you a Messenger confirming that which is with you (of his attributes and description), you will help him and believe in him. Do you agree to that?*. And they all agreed to that. He (and how great a speaker), "Do you agree and affirm that My elect among My creation and My chosen one, Ahmad, is the Seal of the Prophets, the Master of the Messengers, the Beloved of the Lord of the worlds and the proof of Allah upon all His creation? *Do you take My pact upon yourselves?* My covenant. *They said We affirm.* Allah ﷻ responded, *So, bear witness. And I too am a witness with you* that My elect and chosen one from among creation is Ahmad. *So, anyone who turns away after that, they are transgressors.* And that is no boast.

Our Master Jabir b. Abdullah ؓ said,

I said, 'O, Messenger of Allah! May my mother and father be ransomed for you! Inform me of the first thing that Allah ﷻ created before anything else.'

He said, 'O, Jabir! Indeed, Allah ﷻ created, before all things, the light of your Prophet from His own light. And that light began to turn about in the Divine Omnipotence wherever Allah ﷻ willed.

At that time, there was no Tablet, no Pen, no Paradise, No Fire, no Angels, No Heaven, no Earth, no Sun, no Moon, no Jinn and no human being.

Then, when Allah ﷻ willed to create creation, He divided that light into four parts. From the first part, he created the Pen, from the second the Tablet and from the third, the Throne.

Then, He divided the fourth part into four parts. And from the first He created the bearers of the Throne, the second from the Footstool and from the third the rest of the Angels.

Then, He divided the fourth part into four parts. From the first part, He created the Heavens, from the second the Earths and from the third Paradise and the Fire.

Then, He divided the fourth part into four parts. From the first, He created the light of the eyes of the believers, from the second the light of their hearts- which is the gnosis of Allah, and from the third the light of their souls, which is the [word] of Divine Oneness, "There is no god but Allah and Muhammad is His Messenger."

I say, in praise:

> Upon the Chosen and Elect among the whites,
> Be blessing and peace from all, collectively and individually.

O, Allah! Bless our Master Muhammad, the Opener of what was closed, the Seal of what went before, the Helper of the Truth by the Truth and the Guide to Your Straight Path, and his family in accordance with his grandeur and immense worth. And make us, through him, from among his servants, lovers and helpers. And have mercy on us through him. And suffice us against all calamities, disasters, misfortunes, disgraces, worries and anxieties, by Your mercy, o, Most Merciful of the merciful.

When Allah willed to create Adam, the father of mankind and to cause him to obtain all honor and nobility, He created him with His ﷻ hand. And He blew into him of His spirit. And He placed that light in his loins. Then, He commanded the Angels to prostrate to him. He then caused him to abide in Paradise. And the Angels would line up behind him in ranks upon ranks, looking at the light of Muhammad ﷺ. So, Adam said, "My Lord! Why are they linking up behind me in rank after rank? Allah ﷻ said, "They are looking at the light of Muhammad ﷺ, which I will bring out from your back. He is the Seal of the Prophets and Messengers (may Allah's blessings be upon them all). Adam said, "My Lord! Place that light in front of me, so that the Angels will face me and not look at me from behind." So, He placed that light on his forehead. And the Angels would stand in front of Adam in rank upon rank, delighting in the vision of the light of Muhammad ﷺ, which shone on his forehead like the sun and the moon. Adam said, "My Lord! I want there to be, for me, a portion of that light where I can see it." So, Allah ﷻ transferred it to the index finger of his right hand. Whenever Adam would glorify Allah, that light in his index finger would also glorify Allah ﷻ. It is for that reason that the index finger is called *masbahah* [place of glorification]. Then Adam said, "My Lord! Has any part of that light remained?" He replied, "The light of his companions remains." Adam replied, "My Lord! Place it in the rest of my fingers. " So, He placed the light of Abu Bakr in his middle finger, the light of Umar in his ring finger, the light of Uthman in his pinkie and the light of Ali in his thumb.

> O, Allah! Bless our Master Muhammad, the Opener of what was closed, the Seal of what went before, the Helper of the Truth by the Truth and the Guide to Your Straight path, and his family and companions in accordance with his grandeur and immense worth.

> And make us, by his worth, among the chosen and elect of Your victorious army. And cause us to die upon the love of this Elect Prophet. And resurrect us and raise us in the company of his companions in the highest part of *'illiyyin*.

Then, his light continued to be transferred from pure loins, from Adam to Shith to Idris to Ibrahim al-Khalil, to Isma'il to pure wombs. It did not enter any of those wombs by way of fornication. Nor did his forefathers participate in any of the practices of ignorance, from Adam to his father, Abdullah. That was a purification for him. Imam al-Busayri ؓ said:

> You ceased not, in the hidden world, choosing,
> For yourself, mothers and fathers,

> No period occurred between messengers, except,

That Propehts gave glad tidings of you to their people.

> O, Allah! Bless our Master Muhammad, the Openr
> of what was closed, the Seal of what went before, the
> Helper of the Truth by the Truth, and the Guide to
> Your Straight Path, and his family in accordance with
> his grandeur and immense worth.

Until there came the time for the manifestation of his physical body in the physical world and in the world of similitudes, as was written in the sempiternal realm. At that time, shone upon the forehead of Abdullah b. ʿAbd al-Muttalib. It has been narrated by Abdullah, the father of the Messenger of Allah ﷺ that one night he fell asleep in a valley. He dreamt that a chain of light exited from him, having four ends. One end in the east and one in the west. One of them reached up into the sky and one became a green tree upon each of whose leaves was light, and under which the people of the east and the west took shade. When he awoke, he asked the dream interpreters about it. They said, "If you have been truthful, there will come from your loins the one in whom the people of the heavens and the earth will believe, and who will be the Prophet of the end times. And when Allah willed that the light of our Master Muhammad ﷺ should be transferred, He moved the heart of Abdullah b. ʿAbd al-Muttalib to consider marriage, after he had been proposed to by a number of beautiful women who wanted him for themselves. Some of them had even offered him great wealth. And it has been authentically narrated that a woman said to him one day, "Lay upon me and you will have the equal of your ransom in camels." He replied:

> "As for in an unlawful manner, it is better to die first,
> Only the lawful do I seek out,
>
> And the free person protects his honor and religion,
> So, how could you have the matter you are seeking?"

One day, Abdullah said to his mother, "I want you to arrange a marriage for me with a woman of perfect beauty, elegance and splendor, perfect in conduct and high in lineage." She replied, "With great pleasure, my son." Then, she made rounds with the clans of Quraysh and the women of the Arabs. Finding none who pleased her save Aminah b. Wahb. He married her and consummated the marriage. And she became pregnant with the Master of Mankind and the Master of the First and the Last.

Sahl b. Abdullah said, "When Allah willed to create our Master Muhammad ﷺ in the womb of his mother Aminah, on one Friday night of Rajab, he ordered Ridwan, the treasurer of Paradise, to open Firdaws. And a caller called in the heavens and the earth, "Indeed, the hidden, treasured light, from which the Guiding Prophet has been created, has settled this night in the womb of his mother. In him, His creation is completed. And he will emerge among mankind as a bearer of glad tidings and a warner.

Ka'b b. Ahbar ؓ said that on that night, it was called throughout the heavens and their fundaments, and the earth and its regions, that the hidden light from which the Messenger of Allah ﷺ would be created had settled on that night in the womb of his mother. Glad tidings to her! Glad tidings to her! On that day, the idols of the world were overturned. Quraysh had experienced a severe drought. But in that year the earth became green, the trees bore fruit and support came to them from all directions. That year, in which she bore the Messenger of Allah ﷺ was called the year of openings and happiness.

Ibn 'Abbas (may Allah be pleased with father and son) said that among the signs that Amina had become pregnant with the Messenger of Allah ﷺ is that every animal of Quraysh spoke that night, saying, "By the Lord of the Ka'bah! The Messenger of Allah ﷺ has been conceived. He is the Imam of this world and the lamp of its people." All the beds of the rulers of the different kingdoms were overturned that night. The beasts of the east fled to the west with the glad tidings. Likewise, the inhabitants of the sea gave glad tidings to one another. In each of the months in which his mother bore him, a call was made in the earth and in the heavens, "Rejoice. It is nigh that Abu al-Qasim shall appear, auspicious and blessed."

Some of the scholars say that Amina ﷺ related that when she became pregnant with him ﷺ, in the month of Rajab, she saw a man with handsome face and a sweet smell. He was saying, "Welcome to you, o, Muhammad." She said, "I said, 'Who are you?' He replied, 'I am Adam, the father of mankind.' I said, 'What do you want?' He said, 'Rejoice, o, Aminah! You are carrying the Master of human beings and the pride of Rabi'ah and Mudar.'" Aminah said, "In the second month, a man entered upon me saying, 'Peace be upon you, o Messenger of Allah.' I asked, 'Who are you?' He replied, 'I am Shith.' I asked him, 'What do you want?' He replied, 'Rejoice, o, Aminah! You are carrying the supreme interpreter and speaker.' In the third month, a man entered upon me and said, 'Peace be upon you, o, Prophet of Allah!' I asked him, 'Who are you?' He replied, 'I am Idris.' I asked him, 'What do you want?' He replied, 'Rejoice, o, Aminah! You are carrying the Ruler of the Prophets.' In the fourth month, a man entered upon me and said, 'Peace be upon you, o, Beloved of Allah!' I said, 'Who are you?' He said, 'I am Nuh.' I asked him, 'What do you want?' He said, 'Rejoice, o, Aminah! You are carrying the possessor of Divine aid and victories.' In the fifth month, a man entered upon me and said, 'Peace be upon you, o, elect of Allah!' I asked, 'Who are you?' He replied, 'I am Hud.' I asked him, 'What do you want?' He said, 'Rejoice, o, Aminah! You are carrying the greatest intercessor on the appointed day.' In the sixth month, a man entered upon me and said, 'Peace be upon you, o, mercy of Allah!' I asked him, 'Who are you?' He replied, 'I am Ibrahim al-Khalil.' I asked him, 'What do you want?' He replied, 'Rejoice, o, Aminah! You are carrying the Majestic Prophet.' In the seventh month, a man entered upon me saying, 'Peace be upon you, o, you who Allah has chosen.' I said to him, 'Who are you?' He said, 'I am Isma'il, the Sacrificed.' I asked, 'What do you want?' He said, 'Rejoice, o, Aminah! You are carrying the beautiful, superior Prophet.'

In the eighth month, a man entered upon me and said, 'Peace be upon you, o, chosen of Allah!' I asked him, 'Who are you?' He replied, 'I am Musa b. 'Imran.' I asked him, 'What do you want?' He replied, 'Rejoice, o, Aminah! You are carrying the one upon whom the Qur'an will be revealed.' In the ninth month, a man entered upon me and said, 'Peace be upon you, o, Seal of the Messengers of Allah. You have come close, o, Messenger of Allah!' I asked him, 'Who are you?' He replied, 'I am 'Isa b. Maryam.' I asked him, 'What do you want?' He replied, 'Rejoice, o, Aminah! You are carrying the most noble Prophet and greatest Messenger."

> O, Allah! Bless our Master Muhammad, the Opener of what was closed, the Seal of what came before, the Helper of the Truth by the Truth and the Guide to Your Straight path, and his family in accordance with his grandeur and immense worth.

> And give glad tidings to the Prophet of that which we have written and recited. And grant us by means of that, glad tidings with every blinking of an eye and in every moment, o, You whose command is between the *Kaf* and the *Nun*. O, You who but says to a thing, "Be!" And it is.

Ibn Ishaq relates that Aminah ؊ said, 'I did not perceive that I was carrying him. I gained no weight and I had no cravings, as is the case of other women. All that happened was that my cycles ceased, and someone came while I was between sleep and wakefulness and said, 'Do you know that you are carrying the Master of mankind?' Then, he left me alone until the time for my bearing him came. He came to me and said, 'Say: "I have taken refuge in the One from the evil of every jealous person." And name him Muhammad."

It has also been narrated that Allah ؊, as an ennoblement for him ؊ granted all the women of the world male offspring in the year of his birth. Aminah said, "I became pregnant with Muhammad ﷺ on a Friday night in Rajab. And a light entered all the houses of Makkah."

On the first night of the first month she carried him, the cities of Khosrow quaked. On the first night of the second month, all creation was filled with happiness. On the first night of the third month, the river of Sawah ran dry. On the first night of the fourth month, hidden secrets were shown to her. On the first night of the fifth month, the water of the lake of Sawah sunk into the earth. On the first night of the sixth month, the fires were extinguished. On the first night of the seventh month, the cities of Khosrow were split cleft asunder and the crown fell from his head. On the first night of the eight month, he became severely afflicted and agitated. He asked his priests and fortunetellers about it. And they replied, "The time is near for the birth of the son of 'Adnan who is the Prophet of the end times, who has been described in the Torah, the Injil, the Zabur and the Furqan. Upon him the Qur'an will be revealed." On the first night of the ninth month, which is the month of Rabi' al-Awwal, Aminah became elated and felicitous. On the second night, she was given the glad tidings of attaining her hopes. On the third night, it was said to her, "You have carried the one who will establish our praise and thankfulness to us." On the fourth night, she heard the glorification of the Angels in the Heavens. On the fifth night, she saw al-Khalil in a dream. He was saying to her, "Rejoice, O, Aminah, in this majestic Prophet, possessor of grandeur and nobility." On the sixth night, she became completely happy. She lacked nothing and she felt no uneasiness. On the seventh night, the light of satisfaction descended upon her. And her wealth was complete. On the eight night, she heard the tongue of happiness and elation calling out and saying, "O, Aminah! The birth of the light of lights and the full moon of full moons has approached." On the ninth night, her happiness and needlessness became apparent. On the tenth night, the Angels clamored to their Lord with praise, thankfulness and laudation. On the twelfth night she felt the child descend with labor pains and happiness.

O, Allah! Bless our Master Muhammad, the Opener of what was closed, the Seal of what came before, the Helper of the Truth by the Truth and the Guide to Your Straight Path, and his family in accordance with his grandeur and immense worth.

And make this noblest Prophet and greatest Beloved, the food for our spirits and the spirit of our bodies in our religion, in this world and in the Hereafter. And make us among the people with the greatest inheritance from him. And make us among those who witness his splendid countenance forever, in such a way that you never turn us away from it, even for a moment of time. O, Owner of Majesty and Honor!

The Song of the New Spring

اَللَّهُمَّ صَلِّ عَلَى سَيِّدِنَا مُحَمَّدٍ الفَاتِحِ لِمَا أُغْلِقَ وَالخَاتِمِ لِمَا سَبَقَ نَاصِرِ الحَقِّ بِالحَقِّ وَالهَادِي إِلَى صَرَاطِكَ الـمُسْتَقِيمِ وَعَلَى آلِهِ حَقَّ قَدْرِهِ وَمِقْدَارِهِ العَظِيمِ

In the Name of Allah, the Beneficent, the Merciful

O, Allah! Bless our Master Muhammad, the Opener of what was closed, the Seal of what went before, the Helper of the Truth by the Truth and the Guide to Your Straight Path, and his family in accordance with his grandeur and immense worth!

Poems on the Prophetic Birth

All praise is due to Allah! May perfect blessings and peace be upon the one after whom there is no Prophet. This is what our Shaykh and Mediator to Allah, the Lordly *Qutb* and eternal *Tijani Ghawth*, the bringer of the Tijani Flood, would recite when the crescent for the start of the month of the Prophetic Spring, and thereafter during the nights of that month after Wazifa. Likewise, Sidna Baddi al-ʿAlawi 🌺 would do the same. They are as follows:

مِنْ قَبْلِهَا طِبْتَ فِي الظِّلَالِ وَفِي

مُسْتِوْدَعٍ حَيْثُ يُخْصَفُ الْوَرَقُ

ثُمَّ هَبَطْتَ الْبَلَادَ لَا بَشَرٌ

أَنتَ وَلَا مُضْغَةٌ وَلَا عَلَقٌ

مُطَهَّرًا تَرْكَبُ السَّفِينَ وَقَدْ

أَلْجَمَ نَسْرًا وَأَهْلُهُ الْغَرَقُ

وَرَدتَّ نَارَ الْخَلِيلِ مُكْتَتَمًا

تَجُولُ فِيهَا وَلَسْتَ تَحْتَرِقُ

تُنقَلُ مِن صَالِبٍ إِلَى رَحِمٍ
إِذَا مَضَى عَالَمٌ بَدَا طَبَقٌ

حَتَّى احْتَوَى بَيْتَكَ الْمُهَيْمِنُ مِنْ
خِنْدِفٍ عَلْيَاءَ تَحْتَهَا النُّطُقُ

وَأَنتَ لَمَّا وُلِدتَّ أَشْرَقَتِ الْأَرْ
ضُ وَضَاءَتْ بِنُورِكَ الْأُفُقِ

فَنَحْنُ فِي ذَلِكَ الضِّيَاءُ وَفِي النُّو
رِ وَسُبُلِ الرَّشَادِ نَخْتَرِقُ

Min qablihaa tibta fi 'z-zilaali wa fee,
Mustawdi'in haythu yukhsafu 'l-waraqu,

Thumma habatta 'l-bilaada laa basharun,
Anta wa laa mudhatun wa laa 'alaqun,

Mutahharan tarkabu 's-safeena wa qad,
Aljama nasran wa ahlahu 'l-gharaqu,

Wa raddat nara 'l-khaleeli muktataman,
Tajoolu feehaa wa lasta tahtariqun,

Tunqalu min saalibi ilaa rahimin,
Idhaa madaa 'aalamun badaa tabaqu,

Hatta 'htawaa baytaka 'l-Muhayminu min,
Khindifin 'alyaa'a tahtaha 'n-nutuqu,

Wa anta lammaa wulidta ashraqati 'l-ar-
Du wa daa'at bi noorika 'l-ufuqu,

Fa nahnu fee dhalika 'd-diyaa'i wa fi 'n-noo-,
Ri wa subuli 'r-Rashaadi nakhtariqu,

Before it you delighted in the shade and in,
A place where the leaves are sewn together[2],

Then, you descended to the lands, not a man,
Were you, nor piece of flesh nor a clot,

In purity you boarded the ark, Nasr[3] having,
Been restrained and his people drowned,

You entered the fire with the *Khalil*[4], hidden,
Being turned about in it, yet you were not burned,

You were transferred from loins to womb,
When one world passed away, another appeared,

Until the All-Mighty caused you to dwell within,
A lady with unequivocal stature, towering over all others,

And when you were born, the earth was,
Split and the horizons were lit with your light,

And we are in that illumination and light,
Being transported to the path of guidance

---

2   This refers to Paradise [Jannah]
3   Nasr was one of the idols worshipped by the people of Nuh ﷺ
4   Prophet Ibrahim ﷺ

اَللَّهُمَّ إِنَّا نَسْأَلُكَ بِجَاهِ الْمَمْدُوحِ عِنْدَكَ وَالْمَادِحِ أَنْ تُعَظِّمَ حَظَّنَا مِن ذَالِكَ النُّورِ وَالضِّيَاءِ وَأَن تَهْدِيَنَا إِلَى سَبِيلِ الرَّشَادِ آمِينَ

Allaahumma innaa nas'aluka bi jaahi 'l-mamdoohi 'indaka wa 'l-maadihi an tu'azzima hazzanaa min dhaalika 'n-noori wa 'd-diyaa'i wa an tahdiyanaa ilaa sabeeli 'r-Rashaadi. Aameen

O, Allah! We ask You by the status of the one who is praised in Your presence and the one who praises him, to make great our portion of that light and illumination, and to guide us to the path of right guidance. Amin.

يَا مُصْطَفَى مِن قَبْلِ نَشْأَةِ آدَمَ
وَالْكَوْنُ لَمْ تُفْتَحْ لَهُ أَغْلَاقُ

أَيَرُومُ مَخْلُوقٌ ثَنَاءَكَ بَعْدَ مَا
أَثْنَى عَلَى أَخْلَاقِكَ الْخَلَّاقُ

Yaa Mustafaa min qabli nash'ati Aadamin,
Wa 'l-kawnu lam taftah lahu aghlaaqu,

Ayaroomu makhloorun thanaa'aka ba'da maa,
Athnaa 'alaa akhlaaqika 'l-khallaaqu,

O, you who were chosen before the creation of Adam,
Before the locks had been opened for creation,

Can any created being hope to praise you after,
The Creator has praised your character

اَللَّهُمَّ صَلِّ عَلَى سَيِّدِنَا مُحَمَّدِ الْفَاتِحِ لِمَا أُغْلِقَ وَالْخَاتِمِ لِمَا سَبَقَ نَاصِرِ الْحَقِّ بِالْحَقِّ وَالْهَادِي إِلَى صِرَاطِكَ الْمُسْتَقِيمِ وَعَلَى ءَالِهِ حَقَّ قَدْرِهِ وَمِقْدَارِهِ الْعَظِيمِ

Allaahumma salli 'alaa Sayyidinaa Muham-
madini 'l-Faatihi limaa ughliqa wa 'l-Khaatimi
limaa sabaqa Naasiri 'l-haqqi bi 'l-haqqi wa
'l-Haadee ilaa siraatika 'l-mustaqeem wa 'alaa
aalihi haqqa qadrihi wa miqdaarihi 'l-'azeem

O, Allah! Bless our Master Muhammad, the Opener of what was closed, the Seal of what went before, the Helper of the Truth by the Truth and the Guide to Your Straight Path, and his family in accordance with his grandeur and immense worth

---

مَتَى يَبْدُ فِي الدَّاجِ الْبَهِيمِ جَبِينُهُ
يَلُحْ مِثْلَ مِصْبَاحِ الدُّجَى الْمُتَوَقِّدِ

فَمَن كَانَ أَوْ مَنْ ذَا يَكُونُ كَأَحْمَدَ
نِظَامًا لِحَقٍ أَوْ نَكَالًا لِمُلْحِدِ

---

*Mata yabdu fi 'd-duja 'l-baheemi jabeenuhu,
Yaluh mithal misbaahi 'd-duja 'l-muawaqqidi,*

*Fa man kana aw man dhaa yakoonu ka Ahmadin,
Nizaamal li haqqin aw nakaalan li mulhidi*

When his brow appeared in the darkness, pitch black,
It glowed like lit lamps in the opaqueness of night,

And who was or who could be like Ahmad,
In fulfilling rights or punishing a disbeliever

أَغَرَّ عَلَيْهِ بِالنُّبُوَّةِ خَاتِمٌ

$$\text{مِنَ اللهِ بُرْهَانٌ يَلُوحُ وَيَشْهَدُ}$$

$$\text{وَضَمَّ الإِلَهُ اسْمَ النَّبِيِّ إِلَى اسْمِهِ}$$
$$\text{إِذَا قَالَ فِي الْحُمْسِ الْمَؤَذِّنُ اشْهَدُ}$$

$$\text{وَشَقَّ لَهُ مِنِ اسْمِهِ لِيُجِلَّهُ}$$
$$\text{فَذُو الْعَرْشِ مَحْمُودٌ وَهَذَا مُحَمَّدُ}$$

Agharra 'alayhi bi 'n-nubuwwati khaatimun,
Mina 'Llaahi burhaanun yaloohu wa yashhadu,

Wa damma 'l-Ilaahu 'sma 'n-Nabiyyi ila 'smihi,
Idhaa qaala fi 'l-khimsi 'l-mu'adhdhinu ashhadu,

Wa shaqqa lahu mini 'smihi li yujillahu,
Fa Dhu 'l-Arshi Mahmoodun wa haadhaa Muhammadu

He was distinguished in Prophecy by a Seal[5],
From Allah as a proof that shone and was evident,

God joined the name of the Prophet to His own Name,
When the *mu'adhdhin* says the testimony in the call to each prayer,

He gave him a portion of His Name to magnify him,
The Lord of the Throne is *Mahmud* and he is *Muhammad*

---

5   This refers to the seal that was on the Prophet's ﷺ blessed back.

تَحْدِي بِهِ النَّاقَةُ الأَدْمَاءُ مُعْتَجِرًا
بِالْبُرْدِ كَالْبَدْرِ جَلَّى لَيْلَةَ الظُّلَمِ

وَفِي عَطَافَيْهِ أَوْ أَثْنَاءِ بُرْدَتِهِ
مَا يَعْلَمُ اللهُ مِن خَيْرٍ وَمِن كَرَمِ

Takhdee bihi 'n-naaqatu 'l-admaa'u mu'tajiran,
Bi 'l-burdi ka 'l-badri jallaa laylati 'z-zalami,

Wafee 'ataafayhi aw athnaa'i burdatihi,
Maa ya'lami 'Llahu min deenin wa min karami

The brown she-camel carried swiftly his mantle,
Shining like the appearance of the full moon on a dark night,

In his overcoat, or throughout his mantle,
Is that which only Allah knows of good and nobility

إِنَّ الرَّسُولَ لَسَيْفٌ يُسْتَضَاءُ بِهِ
مُهَنَّدٌ مِن سُيُوفِ اللهِ مَسْلُولُ

وَأَبْيَضُ يُسْتَسْقَى الْغَمَامُ بِوَجْهِهِ

ثِمَالُ الْيَتَامَى عِصْمَةٌ لِلْأَرَامِلِ

يَلُوذُ بِهِ الهَلَّاكُ مِنْ آلِ هَاشِمٍ
فَهُمْ عِندَهُ فِي نِعْمَةٍ وَفَوَاضِلِ

مُنَزَّةٌ عَنْ شَرِيكٍ فِي مَحَاسِنِهِ
فَجَوْهَرُ الْحُسْنِ فِيهِ غَيْرُ مُنقَسِمِ

Inna 'r-Rasoola la sayfun yustadaa'u,
Bihi muhannidun min suyoofi 'Llahi masloolu,

Wa abyadu yustasqa 'l-ghamaamu bi wajhihi,
Thimalu 'l-yataamaa 'ismatun li 'l-araamili,

Yaloodhu bihi 'l-hallaaku min Aali Haashimin,
Fa hum 'indahu fee ni'matin wa fawaadili

Munazzahun 'an shareekin fee mahaasinihi
Fa jawharu 'l-husni feehi ghayru munqasimi

Indeed, the Messenger is an unsheathed, Indian,
Sword of Allah that illuminated the way,

A light that dispelled darkness with his countenance,
The comfort of the orphans, a protection for the
widows,

By him, destruction was diverted from the Family of
Hashim,
Such that they are, through him, in blessing and bounty,

He is free of any partner in his beautiful characteristics,
The essence of his beauty is not distributed to anyone

دَعْ مَا ادَّعَتْهُ النَّصَارَى فِي نَبِيِّهِم
وَاحْكُمْ بِمَا شِئْتَ مَدْحًا فِيهِ وَاحْتَكِمِ

وَانْسُبْ إِلَى ذَاتِهِ مَا شِئْتَ مِن شَرَفٍ
وَانسُبْ إِلَى قَدْرِهِ مَا شِئْتَ مِن عِظَمِ

فَإِنَّ فَضْلَ رَسُولِ اللهِ لَيْسَ لَهُ
حَدٌّ فَيُعْرِبُ عَنْهُ نَاطِقٌ بِفَمِ

لَوْ نَاسَبَتْ قَدْرَهُ آيَاتُهُ عِظَمًا
أَحْيَى اسْمُهُ حِينَ يُدْعَى دَارِسَ الرَّمَمِ

لَمْ يَمْتَحِنَّا بِمَا تَعْيَا الْعُقُولُ بِهِ
حِرْصًا عَلَيْنَا فَلَمْ نَرْتَبْ وَلَمْ نَهِمِ

أَعْيَا الوَرَى فَهْمُ مَعْنَاهُ فَلَيْسَ يُرَى
لِلْقُرْبِ وَالْبُعْدِ فِيهِ غَيْرُ مُنْفَحِمِ

كَالشَّمْسِ تَظْهَرُ لِلْعَيْنَيْنِ مِن بَعُدٍ
صَغِيرَةً وَ تُكِلُّ الطَّرْفُ مِنْ أَمَمِ

$$\text{وَكَيْفَ يُدْرِكُ فِي الدُّنْيَا حَقِيقَتَهُ}$$
$$\text{قَوْمٌ نِيَامٌ تَسَلَّوْا عَنْهُ بِالْحُلُمِ}$$

Da' ma 'd-da'athu 'n-nasaaraa fee nabiyyihimi
Wa 'hkum bi maa shi'ta madhan feehi wa 'htakimi,

Wa 'nsub ilaa dhaatihi maa shi'ta min sharafin,
Wa 'nsub ilaa qadrihi maa shi'ta min 'izami,

Fa inna fadla Rasooli 'Llahi laysa lahu,
Haddun fa yu'ribu 'anu naatiqun bi fami,

Law Naasabat qadrahu aayaatuhu 'izamaa,
Ahya 'smuhu heena yud'aa daarisa 'r-rimami,

Lam yamtahinnaa bi maa ta'ya 'l-'uqoolu bhi,
Hirsan 'alaynaa fa lam nartab wa lam nahimi,

A'ya 'l-waraa fahmu ma'naahu fa laysa yaraa,
Fi 'l-qurbi wa 'l-bu'di feehi ghayrun munfahimi,

Ka 'sh-shamsi tazharu li 'l'aynayni min bu'din,
Sagheeratan wa tukillu 't-tarfa min amami,

Wa kayfa yudriku fi 'd-dunyaa haqeeqatahu,
Qasmun niyaamun tasulloo 'anhu bi 'l-hulumi

Leave that which the Christians claimed for their Prophet,
Then, praise him however you will and how you see fit,

Attribute to his being whatever nobility you wish,
Attribute to his status whatever greatness you please,

For, indeed the excellence of the Messenger of Allah has no,
Limit which can be expressed by any speaker or upon any tongue,

If his signs were to match his status in greatness,
His name, if called, would give life to and mend the long forgotten,

We have not been informed of that which the intellect cannot bear,
To protect us from doubting or becoming bewildered,

Human beings are incapable of understanding his reality, So, he is not seen,
By those near or far, except that they are incapacitated,

Just as the sun appears to the eyes, from a distance,
As small, even if one's incapacity to look at it should mean that it is close,

How should his reality be perceived in this world,
By a people who are asleep and distracted from him by a dream

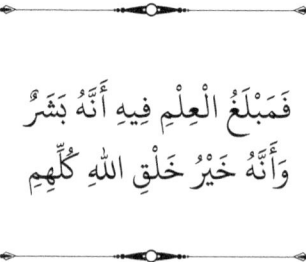

*Fa mablaghu 'l-'ilmi feehi annahu basharun,
Wa annahu khayru khalqi 'Llahi kullihimi*

Thus, the extent of our knowledge is that he is a man,
And that he is the best of all Allah's creation

مَن ذَا الَّذِي مَا سَاءَ قَطُّ
وَمَن لَّهُ الْحُسْنَى فَقَطْ

مُحَمَّدٌ الْهَادِي الذِي
عَلَيْهِ جِبْرِيلُ هَبَطْ

*Man dha 'lladhee maa sawaa'a qat,
Wa man lahu 'l-husnaa faqat,*

*Muhammadu 'l-Haadi 'lladhee,
'Alayhi Jibreelu habat*

Who is the one that has done no evil at all,
Who has done only good,

Muhammad, the Guide to whom,
Jibril descended

مُحَمَّدٌ بَشَرٌ لَا كَالْبَشَرِ
بَلْ هُوَ كَالْيَاقُوتِ بَيْنَ الْحَجَرْ

Muhammadan basharun laa ka 'l-bashari,
Bal huwa ka '-yaaqooti bayna 'l-hajari

Muhammad is a man, but not like other men,
Nay, he is like a ruby among stones

اَللّٰهُمَّ صَلِّ عَلَى مَنْ فَاتِحِيَّتُهُ لِبَدِيعِ الْإِيجَادِ بَرَاعَةُ الْإِسْتِهْلَالِ وَمَنْ خَاتِمِيَّتُهُ بَرَاعَةُ الْمَخْتَمِ وَالْكَمَالِ. اَللّٰهُمَّ صَلِّ عَلَى سَيِّدِنَا مُحَمَّدٍ بَحْرِ أَنْوَارِكَ وَمَعْدِنِ أَسْرَارِكَ وَلِسَانِ حُجَّتِكَ وَعُرُوسِ مَمْلَكَتِكَ وَإِمَامِ حَضْرَتِكَ وَطِرَازِ مُلْكِكَ وَخَزَائِنِ رَحْمَتِكَ وَطَرِيقِ شَرِيعَتِكَ الْمُتَلَذِّذِ بِتَوْحِيدِكَ إِنْسَانِ عَيْنِ الْوُجُودِ وَالسَّبَبِ كُلِّ مَوْجُودٍ عَيْنِ أَعْيَانِ خَلْقِكَ الْمُتَقَدِّم مِنْ نُورِ ضِيَآئِكَ صَلَاةً تَدُومُ بِدَوَامِكَ وَتَبْقَى بِبَقَآئِكَ صَلَاةً لَا مُنْتَهَى لَهَا دُونَ عِلْمِكَ صَلَاةً تُرْضِيكَ وَتُرْضِيهِ وَتَرْضَى بِهَا عَنَّا وَعَنْ وَالِدَيْنَا وَعَنْ أَزْوَاجِنَا وَذُرِّيَّاتِنَا يَا رَبَّ الْعَالَمِينَ آمين

Allaahumma salli 'alaa man faatihiyyatuhu li badee'i 'l-eejaadi baraa'ati 'l-istihlaali wa man khaatimiyyatuhu baraa'ati 'l-mukhtimi wa 'l-kamaal.

Allaahumma salli 'alaa Sayyidinaa Muhammadin bahri anwaarika wa ma'dani asraarika wa lisaani hujjatika wa 'uroosi mamlakatika wa imaami hadratika wa tiraazi mulkika wa khazaa'ini rahmatika wa tareeqi sharee'atika 'l-mutaladhdhidhi bi tawheedika insaanu 'ayni 'l-wujoodi wa 's-sababu fee kulli mawjoodin 'ayni a'yaani khalqika 'l-mutaqaddimu min noori diyaa'ika salaatan tadoomu bi dawaamika wa tabqaa bi baqaa'ika salaatan laa muntahaa lahaa doona 'ilmika salaatan turdeeka wa turdeehi wa tardaa bihaa 'annaa wa 'an waalideenaa wa ashyaakhinaa wa azwaajinaa wa dhurriyyaatinaa yaa Rabba 'l-'aalameen

---

O, Allah! Bless the one whose opening of unprecedented being is the most excellent beginning, and whose sealing is the most excellent ending and perfection. O, Allah! Bless our Master Muhammad, the ocean of Your lights, the treasury of Your secrets, the tongue of Your proof, the bridegroom of Your kingdom, the *Imam* of Your presence, the model of the treasuries of Your mercy, the medium of Your Sacred Law who delights in Your unicity, the essence of being, the cause of every created thing, the essential essence of Your creation, who proceed from Your illuminating light, with an endless and perpetual blessing as long as You remain, with a blessing which has no limit in Your knowledge, and with a blessing that will satisfy You, satisfy him and by which You will be satisfied with us, our children, our Shaykhs, our wives and our offspring, o, Lord of the worlds!

لِي سَادَةٌ مِن عِزِّهِمْ
أَقْدَامُهُمْ فَوْقَ الْجِبَاهْ

اِن لَمْ أَكُن مِنْهُمْ فَلِي
بِحُبِّهِمْ عِزٌّ وَجَاهْ

فَبِجَاهِهِمْ وَبِعِزِّهِمْ
طَيِّبْ لَنَا عَيْشَ الْحَيَاهْ

وَاخْتِمْ لَنَا بِالْخَيْرِ يَا
مَن لَا لَنَا رَبٌّ سِوَاهْ

Lee saadatun min 'izzihim,
Aqdaamuhum fawqa 'l-jibaah,

In lam akun minhum fa lee,
Bi hubbihim 'izzun wa jaah,

Bi jaahihim wa 'izzihim,
Tayyib lanaa 'aysha 'l-hayaah,

Wa 'khtim lanaa bi 'l-khayri yaa,
Man laa lanaa rabbun siwaah

I have masters, whose nobility is such,
That their feet are above the foreheads of mankind,

If I am not among them, then I have,
Through love of them, nobility and status,

So, by their status and nobility,
Better our lifestyles,

And seal them with goodness, o,
You who are our only Lord

اَللَّهُمَّ صَلِّ عَلَى مَنْ فَاتِحِيَّتُهُ لِبَدِيعِ الإِيجَادِ بَرَاعَةِ الاِسْتِهْلَالِ وَمَنْ خَاتِمِيَّتُهُ بَرَاعَةُ الـمُخْتَمِ وَالكَمَالِ،

اَللَّهُمَّ إِنَّا نَسْأَلُكَ بِفَاتِحِيَّةِ الفَاتِحِ الفَتْحَ التَّامَّ،
وَبِخَاتِمِيَّةِ الخَاتِمِ حُسْنَ الخِتَامِ،

Allaahumma salli 'alaa man faatihiyyatuhu li badee'i 'l-eejaadi baraa'ati 'l-istihlaali wa man khaatimiyyatuhu baraa'ati 'l-mukhtimi wa 'l-kamaal.

Allaahummaa innaaa nas'aluka bi faatihiyyati 'l-Faaatihi 'l-fatha 't-taammi wa bi khaatimi-yyati 'l-khaatimi husna 'l-khitaam

O, Allah! Bless the one whose opening of unprecedented being is the most excellent beginning, and whose sealing is the most excellent ending and perfection. O, Allah! We ask You by the opening of the Opener a complete opening, and by the sealing of the Seal and beautiful ending

Poem in Praise of the Messenger of Allah ﷺ

قال الشيخ بدّ بن سيدنا :

تَهْنِئَةُ الرَّبِيعِ ، بِمَدْحَةِ الشَّفِيعِ ، بِالـمَنْطِقِ الْبَدِيعِ ،
أَبْغِي بِهَا مُؤَمَّلِي

يَا رَبَّنَا صَلِّ عَلَى خَيْرِ الْأَنَامِ مَنْ عَلَا عَلَى السَّمَوَاتِ الْعُلَى
بِإِذْنِ رَبِّهِ الْعَلِيِّ

تَهْنِئَةُ الرَّبِيعِ ، بِمَدْحَةِ الشَّفِيعِ ، بِالـمَنْطِقِ الْبَدِيعِ ،
أَبْغِي بِهَا مُؤَمَّلِي

أَهْلًا بِشَهْرِ الْمَوْلِدِ شَهْرِ الْعُلَا وَالسَّوْدَدِ شَهْرِ النَّبِيِّ أَحْمَدِ
شَهْرِ رَبِيعِ الْأَوَّلِ

تَهْنِئَةُ الرَّبِيعِ ، بِمَدْحَةِ الشَّفِيعِ ، بِالـمَنْطِقِ الْبَدِيعِ ،
أَبْغِي بِهَا مُؤَمَّلِي

قَدْ خُصَّ بِالرَّبِيعِ إِذْ كَانَ كَالرَّبِيعِ لِلْأَرْضِ وَالشَّفِيعِ بِكُلِّ خَطْبٍ مُعْضِلِ

تَهْنِئَةُ الرَّبِيعِ، بِمَدْحَةِ الشَّفِيعِ، بِالْمَنْطِقِ الْبَدِيعِ، أَبْغِي بِهَا مُؤَمَّلِي

أَهْلًا بِشَهْرِ الْفَرَحَ شَهْرِ ذَهَابِ التَّرَحَ وَفَخْرِنَا وَالْمَرَحَ شَهْرِ النَّبِيِّ الْأَفْضَلِ

تَهْنِئَةُ الرَّبِيعِ، بِمَدْحَةِ الشَّفِيعِ، بِالْمَنْطِقِ الْبَدِيعِ، أَبْغِي بِهَا مُؤَمَّلِي

شَهْرِ الْفَلَاحِ وَالسُّرُورْ شَهْرٍ بِهِ سَادَ الدُّهُورْ مُوَشَّحٍ بَيْنَ الشُّهُورْ مَتَوَّجٍ مُكَلَّلِ

تَهْنِئَةُ الرَّبِيعِ، بِمَدْحَةِ الشَّفِيعِ، بِالْمَنْطِقِ الْبَدِيعِ، أَبْغِي بِهَا مُؤَمَّلِي

أَهْلًا بِشَهْرِ الْفَاتِحِ اِغْلَاقِ كَوْنِ الْفَاتِحِ مَنْ خُصَّ بِالْفَوَاتِحِ وَحَازَ خَتْمَ الْمِلَلِ

تَهْنِئَةُ الرَّبِيعِ، بِمَدْحَةِ الشَّفِيعِ، بِالْمَنْطِقِ الْبَدِيعِ، أَبْغِي بِهَا مُؤَمَّلِي

أَهْلًا بِشَهْرِ الْخَاتِمِ شَهْرِ نَبِيٍّ قَاسِمٍ وَفَاتِحٍ وَخَاتِمٍ وَآخِرٍ وَأَوَّلِ

تَهْنِئَةُ الرَّبِيعِ ، بِمَدْحَةِ الشَّفِيعِ ، بِالـمَنْطِقِ الْبَدِيعِ ، أَبْغِي بِهَا مُؤَمَّلِي

أَهْلًا بِشَهْرِ النَّاصِرِ لِلْحَقِّ شَهْرِ الآمِرِ بِالْعُرْفِ شَهْرِ الظَّاهِرِ بِكُلِّ وَصْفٍ أَكْمَلِ

تَهْنِئَةُ الرَّبِيعِ ، بِمَدْحَةِ الشَّفِيعِ ، بِالـمَنْطِقِ الْبَدِيعِ ، أَبْغِي بِهَا مُؤَمَّلِي

أَهْلًا بِشَهْرِ الْهَادِي لِمَنهَجِ الرَّشَادِ وَقَائِدٍ وَحَادِي إِلَى الطَّرِيقِ الْأَمْثَلِ

تَهْنِئَةُ الرَّبِيعِ ، بِمَدْحَةِ الشَّفِيعِ ، بِالـمَنْطِقِ الْبَدِيعِ ، أَبْغِي بِهَا مُؤَمَّلِي

أَهْلًا بِشَهْرِ السَّيِّدِ لْأَحْمَرٍ وَأَسْوَدٍ مَنْ حَازَ سَبْقَ السُّؤْدَدِ يَوْم اعْتِذَارِ الرُّسُلِ

تَهْنِئَةُ الرَّبِيعِ ، بِمَدْحَةِ الشَّفِيعِ ، بِالـمَنْطِقِ الْبَدِيعِ ، أَبْغِي بِهَا مُؤَمَّلِي

وَقَدْ كَفَاهَا كُلَّهَا أَعْبَاءَهَا وَكَلَّهَا بِقَوْلِهِ أَنَا لَهَا عِندَ اشْتِدَادِ الْوَجَلِ

تَهْنِئَةُ الرَّبِيعِ، بِمَدْحَةِ الشَّفِيعِ، بِالـمَنْطِقِ الْبَدِيعِ، أَبْغِي بِهَا مُؤَمَّلِي

فَيَالَهَا مِن خُطَّةْ جَوَابُهُ فِي الْخُطَّةْ مِن رَبِّهِ سَلْ تُعْطَهْ وَاشْفَعْ لَدَيْنَا تُقْبَلِ

تَهْنِئَةُ الرَّبِيعِ، بِمَدْحَةِ الشَّفِيعِ، بِالـمَنْطِقِ الْبَدِيعِ، أَبْغِي بِهَا مُؤَمَّلِي

أَهْلًا بِشَهْرِ الْمُصْطَفَى صَفْوَةِ كُلِّ مُصْطَفَى وَخَيْرِ عَبْدٍ قَدْ صَفَى مِن مَلَكٍ أَوْ مُرْسَلِ

تَهْنِئَةُ الرَّبِيعِ بِمَدحة الشفيع بالـمنطق البديع أبغي بها مؤملي

وَشَهْرِ خَيْرِ الْخَلْقِ شَهْرِ جَمِيلِ الْخَلْقِ شَهْرِ عَظِيمِ الْخَلْقِ فِي الْمُحْكَمِ الْمُنَزَّلِ

تَهْنِئَةُ الرَّبِيعِ، بِمَدْحَةِ الشَّفِيعِ، بِالـمَنْطِقِ الْبَدِيعِ، أَبْغِي بِهَا مُؤَمَّلِي

شَهْرِ الذِي ءَاثَرَهُ إِلَهُهُ وَاخْتَارَهُ مِن حُبِّهِ خَيَّرَهُ عِندَ انقِضَاءِ الْأَجَلِ

تَهْنِئَةُ الرَّبِيعِ، بِمَدْحَةِ الشَّفِيعِ، بِالـمَنْطِقِ الْبَدِيعِ، أَبْغِي بِهَا مُؤَمَّلِي

شَهْرِ الذِي مَا سَآءَ قَطُّ وَمَن لَهُ الْحُسْنَى فَقَطْ عَلَيْهِ جِبْرِيلُ هَبَطْ بِكُلِّ نُورٍ مُعْتَلِ

تَهْنِئَةُ الرَّبِيعِ، بِمَدْحَةِ الشَّفِيعِ، بِالـمَنْطِقِ الْبَدِيعِ، أَبْغِي بِهَا مُؤَمَّلِي

أَهْلًا بِلَيْلٍ اثَنَىْ عَشَرْ فِيهِ وَيَوْمِهِ الْأَغَرْ وَطِيبِ ذَالِكَ السَّحَرْ وَنُورِ أُفْقِهِ الْجَلِيِّ

تَهْنِئَةُ الرَّبِيعِ، بِمَدْحَةِ الشَّفِيعِ، بِالـمَنْطِقِ الْبَدِيعِ، أَبْغِي بِهَا مُؤَمَّلِي

أَهْلًا بِكُلِّ مَا ظَهَرْ مِن خَارِقٍ يُعْيِي الَفِكْرِ فِيهِ كَرَفْعِهِ الْبَصَرْ إِلَى مَقَامِهِ الْعَلِيِّ

تَهْنِئَةُ الرَّبِيعِ، بِمَدْحَةِ الشَّفِيعِ، بِالـمَنْطِقِ الْبَدِيعِ، أَبْغِي بِهَا مُؤَمَّلِي

وَمَا رَأَتْهُ مِن عَجَبٍ آمِنَةٌ حِينَ نَصَبْ سَبَابَةً ثُمَّ اقْتَرَبْ بِسَجْدَةِ الْمُبْتَهِلْ

تَهْنِئَةُ الرَّبِيعِ ، بِمَدْحَةِ الشَّفِيعِ ، بِالْـمَنْطِقِ الْبَدِيعِ ، أَبْغِي بِهَا مُؤَمَّلِي

كَمَا تَدَلَّى الزُّهْرُ كَمَا تَرَاءَى الْقَصْرُ فِيهِ وَحَلَّ الْكَسْرُ بِالصَّنَمِ الْمُجَدَّلِ

تَهْنِئَةُ الرَّبِيعِ ، بِمَدْحَةِ الشَّفِيعِ ، بِالْـمَنْطِقِ الْبَدِيعِ ، أَبْغِي بِهَا مُؤَمَّلِي

وَغَاضَتِ الْبِحَارُ وَجَفَّتِ الْأَنْهَارُ مِنْ أَجْلِهِ وَالنَّارُ قَدْ طَفِئَتْ مِنْ خَجَلِ

تَهْنِئَةُ الرَّبِيعِ ، بِمَدْحَةِ الشَّفِيعِ ، بِالْـمَنْطِقِ الْبَدِيعِ ، أَبْغِي بِهَا مُؤَمَّلِي

وَجِنُّهُمْ فِي نَكَدٍ لِرَمْيِهَا بِالرَّصَدِ وَعَزْلِهَا عَن مَقْعَدِ مِنْ أَجْلِ خَيْرِ الرُّسُلِ

تَهْنِئَةُ الرَّبِيعِ ، بِمَدْحَةِ الشَّفِيعِ ، بِالْـمَنْطِقِ الْبَدِيعِ ، أَبْغِي بِهَا مُؤَمَّلِي

وَرَنَّةِ الشَّيْطَانِ جَرَّا عَظِيمُ الشَّأْنِ مِن أَوْضَحِ الْبُرْهَانِ لِعُظْمِ مَا بِهِ ابْتُلِي

تَهْنِئَةُ الرَّبِيعِ ، بِمَدْحَةِ الشَّفِيعِ ، بِالـمَنْطِقِ الْبَدِيعِ ، أَبْغِي بِهَا مُؤَمَّلِي

قَدْ مَنَّ ذُو الْإِفْضَالِ بِأَفْضَلِ الرِّجَالِ فِي أَفْضَلِ اللَّيَالِي بِالْبَلَدِ الْمُفَضَّلِ

تَهْنِئَةُ الرَّبِيعِ ، بِمَدْحَةِ الشَّفِيعِ ، بِالـمَنْطِقِ الْبَدِيعِ ، أَبْغِي بِهَا مُؤَمَّلِي

أَهْلًا بِيَوْمِ عِيدٍ مَا مِثْلُهُ مِن عِيدٍ قَدْ حَلَّ فِي الْمَوْلُودِ فِيهِ مَحَلَّ زُحَلِ

تَهْنِئَةُ الرَّبِيعِ ، بِمَدْحَةِ الشَّفِيعِ ، بِالـمَنْطِقِ الْبَدِيعِ ، أَبْغِي بِهَا مُؤَمَّلِي

وَسَابِعُ الْوِلَادَةِ وَمَا أَتَاهُ السَّادَةُ مِن وِفْقِ مَا أَرَادَهُ إِلَهُهُ فِي الْأَزَلِ

تَهْنِئَةُ الرَّبِيعِ ، بِمَدْحَةِ الشَّفِيعِ ، بِالـمَنْطِقِ الْبَدِيعِ ، أَبْغِي بِهَا مُؤَمَّلِي

أَهْلًا بِيَوْمٍ سُمِّيَ مُحَمَّدًا خَيْرَ اسْمٍ رَمْزًا لِمَعْنَى الْإِسْمِ مِن جَدِّهِ لِيَنجَلِ

تَهْنِئَةُ الرَّبِيعِ ، بِمَدْحَةِ الشَّفِيعِ ، بِالمَنْطِقِ الْبَدِيعِ ، أَبْغِي بِهَا مُؤَمَّلِي

بِحَمْدِ الْأَوَّلِينَا لَهُ وَالْآخِرِينَا فَكَانَ ذَا يَقِينًا مِنَ الْكَرِيمِ الْمُفْضَلِ

تَهْنِئَةُ الرَّبِيعِ ، بِمَدْحَةِ الشَّفِيعِ ، بِالمَنْطِقِ الْبَدِيعِ ، أَبْغِي بِهَا مُؤَمَّلِي

أَهْلًا بِيَوْمِ الْإِثْنَيْنِ مَوْلِدِ ثَانِي اثْنَيْنِ مَبْعَثِ سِرِّ الْكَوْنِ مَقْدَمِهِ الْمُبَجَّلِ

تَهْنِئَةُ الرَّبِيعِ ، بِمَدْحَةِ الشَّفِيعِ ، بِالمَنْطِقِ الْبَدِيعِ ، أَبْغِي بِهَا مُؤَمَّلِي

اكْرِمْ بِشَهْرِ الْعَجَمِ ابْرِيلَ شَهْرِ الْكَرَمِ أَكْرِمْ بِأَرْضِ الحَرَمِ مَوْلِدِ خَيْرِ مُرْسَلِ

تَهْنِئَةُ الرَّبِيعِ ، بِمَدْحَةِ الشَّفِيعِ ، بِالمَنْطِقِ الْبَدِيعِ ، أَبْغِي بِهَا مُؤَمَّلِي

اَكْرِمْ بِيَوْمٍ صَارَا عِشْرِينَ وَاسْتَنَارًا لِمَنْ حَوَى الْفَخَارَا وَغُفْرَةً مِن مَنزِلِ

تَهْنِئَةُ الرَّبِيعِ، بِمَدْحَةِ الشَّفِيعِ، بِالـمَنْطِقِ الْبَدِيعِ، أَبْغِي بِهَا مُؤَمَّلِي

اَكْرِمْ بِشَهْرِ النِّيسَانِ مَوْلِدِ خَيْرِ إِنسَانِ قُدْوَةِ أَهْلِ الْإِحْسَانِ وِالْكَامِلِ الْمُكَمَّلِ

تَهْنِئَةُ الرَّبِيعِ، بِمَدْحَةِ الشَّفِيعِ، بِالـمَنْطِقِ الْبَدِيعِ، أَبْغِي بِهَا مُؤَمَّلِي

قَدْ تَمَّتِ اللَّئَالِي فِي عِدَّةِ اللَّيَالِي بِزِينَةِ الْمَعَالِي كَالْجَوْهَرِ الْمُفَضَّلِ

تَهْنِئَةُ الرَّبِيعِ، بِمَدْحَةِ الشَّفِيعِ، بِالـمَنْطِقِ الْبَدِيعِ، أَبْغِي بِهَا مُؤَمَّلِي

تَهْنِئَةُ الرَّبِيعِ بِمَدْحَةِ الشَّفِيعِ بِالـمَنْطِقِ الْبَدِيعِ أَبْغَي بِهَا مُؤَمَّلِي

تَهْنِئَةُ الرَّبِيعِ، بِمَدْحَةِ الشَّفِيعِ، بِالـمَنْطِقِ الْبَدِيعِ، أَبْغِي بِهَا مُؤَمَّلِي

أَبْغِي بِهَا الْجَمْعَ بِهِ يَوْمًا وَنَيْلَ قُرْبِهِ وَفَضْلَ حُبِّ رَبِّهِ وَمَنْ رِضَاهُ أَمَلِي

تَهْنِئَةُ الرَّبِيعِ، بِمَدْحَةِ الشَّفِيعِ، بِالـمَنْطِقِ الْبَدِيعِ، أَبْغِي بِهَا مُؤَمَّلِي

وَالْخَتْمَ لِي بِالْحُسْنَى وَالْجَمْعَ لِي فِي الْحُسْنَى لَدَى الْمَقَرِّ الْأَسْنَى مَعَ الرَّفِيقِ الْأَفْضَلِ

تَهْنِئَةُ الرَّبِيعِ، بِمَدْحَةِ الشَّفِيعِ، بِالـمَنْطِقِ الْبَدِيعِ، أَبْغِي بِهَا مُؤَمَّلِي

وَكُنْ لَنَا وَلِيًّا وَنَاصِرًا حَفِيًّا لَا نَخْتَشِي غَوِيًّا بِجَاهِ عَبْدِكَ الْعَلِيّ

تَهْنِئَةُ الرَّبِيعِ، بِمَدْحَةِ الشَّفِيعِ، بِالـمَنْطِقِ الْبَدِيعِ، أَبْغِي بِهَا مُؤَمَّلِي

صَلَّى وَسَلَّمَ الْإِلَهُ عَلَيْهِ أَفْضَلَ الصَّلَاةِ مَا دَامَ كَوْنُهُ إِلَهً مِنْ أَبَدٍ لِأَزَلِ

تَهْنِئَةُ الرَّبِيعِ، بِمَدْحَةِ الشَّفِيعِ، بِالـمَنْطِقِ الْبَدِيعِ، أَبْغِي بِهَا مُؤَمَّلِي

وَءَالِهِ وَصَحْبِهِ وَزَوْجِهِ وَحِزْبِهِ وَكُلِّ ءَالِ حُبِّهِ مَعَ السَّلَامِ الْأَكْمَلِ

تَهْنِئَةُ الرَّبِيعِ، بِمَدْحَةِ الشَّفِيعِ، بِالـمَنْطِقِ الْبَدِيعِ، أَبْغِي بِهَا مُؤَمَّلِي

انتهى

Transliteration of Poem

Tahni'atu 'r-Rabi'i; Bi madhati 'sh-Shafee'i,
Bi 'l-mantiqi 'l-badee'i; Abghee bihaa mu'ammalee

Yaa Rabbanaa salli 'alaa; Khayri 'l-anami man 'alaa,
'Ala 's-samaawaati 'l-'ulaa; Bi idhni Rabbihi 'l-'Aliyy,

Tahni'atu 'r-Rabi'i; Bi madhati 'sh-Shafee'i,
Bi 'l-mantiqi 'l-badee'i; Abghee bihaa mu'ammalee

Ahlan bi shahri 'l-mawlidi; Shahri 'l-'ulaa wa 's-su'dadi,
Shahri 'n-Nabiyyi Ahmadi; Shahri Rabee'I 'l-awwali,

Tahni'atu 'r-Rabi'i; Bi madhati 'sh-Shafee'i,
Bi 'l-mantiqi 'l-badee'i; Abghee bihaa mu'ammalee

Qad khussa bi 'r-rabee'i; Idh kaana ka 'r-rabee'I,
Li 'l-ardi wa 'sh-Shafee'i; Li kulli khatbin mu'dili,

Tahni'atu 'r-Rabi'i; Bi madhati 'sh-Shafee'i,
Bi 'l-mantiqi 'l-badee'i; Abghee bihaa mu'ammalee

Ahlan bi shahri 'l-farahi; Shahr dhahaabi 't-tarahi,
Wa fakhrinaa wa 'l-marahi; Shahri 'n-Nabiyyi 'l-Afdali,

Tahni'atu 'r-Rabi'i; Bi madhati 'sh-Shafee'i,
Bi 'l-mantiqi 'l-badee'i; Abghee bihaa mu'ammalee

Shahri 'l-falaahi wa 's-suroor; Shahrin bihi saada 'd-duhoor,
Mutawashshihin bayna 'sh-shuhoor; Mutawajjin mukallali,

Tahni'atu 'r-Rabi'i; Bi madhati 'sh-Shafee'i,
Bi 'l-mantiqi 'l-badee'i; Abghee bihaa mu'ammalee

Ahlan bi sharhi 'l-Faatihi; Aghlaqi kawni 'l-Faatihi,
Man khussa bi 'l-fawaatihi; Wa haaza khatma 'l-milali,

Tahni'atu 'r-Rabi'i; Bi madhati 'sh-Shafee'i,
Bi 'l-mantiqi 'l-badee'i; Abghee bihaa mu'ammalee

Ahlan bi shahri 'l-Khaatimi; Shahri Nabiyyin Qaasimi,
Wa Faatihi wa Khaatimi; Wa Aakhirin wa Awwali,

Tahni'atu 'r-Rabi'i; Bi madhati 'sh-Shafee'i,
Bi 'l-mantiqi 'l-badee'i; Abghee bihaa mu'ammalee

Ahlan bi shahri 'n-Naasiri; Li 'l-haqqi shahri 'l-Aamiri,
Bi 'l-'urfi shahri 'z-zaahiri; Bi kulli wasfin akmali,

Tahni'atu 'r-Rabi'i; Bi madhati 'sh-Shafee'i,
Bi 'l-mantiqi 'l-badee'i; Abghee bihaa mu'ammalee

Ahlan bi shahri 'l-Haadee; Li manhaaji 'r-Rashaadi,
Wa qaa'idin wa haadi; Ila 't-tareeqi 'l-amthali,

Tahni'atu 'r-Rabi'i; Bi madhati 'sh-Shafee'i,
Bi 'l-mantiqi 'l-badee'i; Abghee bihaa mu'ammalee

Ahlan bi shahri 's-Sayyidi; Li ahmarin wa aswadin,
Man haaza sabqa 's-soodad; Yawma 'tidhari 'r-rusuli,

Tahni'atu 'r-Rabi'i; Bi madhati 'sh-Shafee'i,
Bi 'l-mantiqi 'l-badee'i; Abghee bihaa mu'ammalee

Wa qad kafaahaa kullahaa; A'baa'ahaa wa kallahaa
Bi qawlihi ana lahaa; 'Inda 'shtidaadi 'l-wajali,

Tahni'atu 'r-Rabi'i; Bi madhati 'sh-Shafee'i,
Bi 'l-mantiqi 'l-badee'i; Abghee bihaa mu'ammalee

Fa yaa lahaa min khittah; Jawaabuhu fi 'l-hittah,
Min Rabbihi sal tu'tah; Wa 'shfa' ladaynaa tuqbali,

Tahni'atu 'r-Rabi'i; Bi madhati 'sh-Shafee'i,
Bi 'l-mantiqi 'l-badee'i; Abghee bihaa mu'ammalee

Ahlan bi shahri 'l-Mustafaa; Safwati kulli Mustafaa,
Wa Khayri 'abdin qad safaa; Min Malakin wa Mursalin,

Tahni'atu 'r-Rabi'i; Bi madhati 'sh-Shafee'i,
Bi 'l-mantiqi 'l-badee'i; Abghee bihaa mu'ammalee

Wa shahru khayri 'l-khalqi; Shahrun jameelu 'l-khulqi,
Shahrun 'azeemu 'l-khulqi; Fi 'l-Muhkami 'l-Munazzali,

Tahni'atu 'r-Rabi'i; Bi madhati 'sh-Shafee'i,
Bi 'l-mantiqi 'l-badee'i; Abghee bihaa mu'ammalee

Shahru 'lladhee aatharahu; Ilaahuhu wa 'khtaarahu,
Man hibbuhu khayyarahu; 'Inda 'nqidaa'i 'l-ajali,

Tahni'atu 'r-Rabi'i; Bi madhati 'sh-Shafee'i,
Bi 'l-mantiqi 'l-badee'i; Abghee bihaa mu'ammalee

Shahru 'lladhee maa saa'a qat; Wa man lahu 'l-husnaa faqat,
'Alayhi Jibreelu habat; Bi kulli noorin mu'talee,

Tahni'atu 'r-Rabi'i; Bi madhati 'sh-Shafee'i,
Bi 'l-mantiqi 'l-badee'i; Abghee bihaa mu'ammalee

Ahlan bi layli 'thnay 'ashar; Feehi wa yawmihi 'l-aghar,
Wa teebi dhaalika 's-sahar; Wa noori ufqihi 'l-jalee,

Tahni'atu 'r-Rabi'i; Bi madhati 'sh-Shafee'i,
Bi 'l-mantiqi 'l-badee'i; Abghee bihaa mu'ammalee

Ahlan bi kulli maa zahar; Min khaariqin yu'yi 'l-fikar,
Feehi ka raf'ihi 'l-basar; Ilaa maqaamihi 'l-'alee,

Tahni'atu 'r-Rabi'i; Bi madhati 'sh-Shafee'i,
Bi 'l-mantiqi 'l-badee'i; Abghee bihaa mu'ammalee

Wa maa ra'athu min 'ajab; Aaminatun heena nasab,
Sabbabatan thumma 'qtaraba; Bi sajdati 'l-mubtahili,

Tahni'atu 'r-Rabi'i; Bi madhati 'sh-Shafee'i,
Bi 'l-mantiqi 'l-badee'i; Abghee bihaa mu'ammalee

Kamaa tadalla 'zahru; Kamaa taraa'a 'l-qasru,
Feehi wa halla 'l-kasru; Bi 'd-danami 'l-mujaddali,

Tahni'atu 'r-Rabi'i; Bi madhati 'sh-Shafee'i,
Bi 'l-mantiqi 'l-badee'i; Abghee bihaa mu'ammalee

Wa ghaadati 'l-bihaaru; Wa jaffati 'l-anhaaru,
Min ajlihi wa 'n-naaru; Qad tafi'at min khajali,

Tahni'atu 'r-Rabi'i; Bi madhati 'sh-Shafee'i,
Bi 'l-mantiqi 'l-badee'i; Abghee bihaa mu'ammalee

Wa jinnuhum fee nakadi; Li ramyihaa bi 'r-rasadi,
Wa 'azlihaa 'an maq'adi; Min ajli khayri 'r-rusuli,

Tahni'atu 'r-Rabi'i; Bi madhati 'sh-Shafee'i,
Bi 'l-mantiqi 'l-badee'i; Abghee bihaa mu'ammalee

Wa rannati 'sh-Shaytaani; Jarraa 'azeemi 'sh-shaani,
Min awdahi 'l-burhaani; Li 'uzmi maa bihi 'btulee,

Tahni'atu 'r-Rabi'i; Bi madhati 'sh-Shafee'i,
Bi 'l-mantiqi 'l-badee'i; Abghee bihaa mu'ammalee

Qad manna dhu 'l-ifdaali; Bi afdali 'r-rijaali,
Fee afdali 'l-layaalee; Fi 'l-baladi 'l-mufaddali,

Tahni'atu 'r-Rabi'i; Bi madhati 'sh-Shafee'i,
Bi 'l-mantiqi 'l-badee'i; Abghee bihaa mu'ammalee

Ahlan bi yami 'eedi; Maa mithluhu min 'eedi,
Qad halla bi 'l-mawloodi; Feehi mahallu zuhali,

Tahni'atu 'r-Rabi'i; Bi madhati 'sh-Shafee'i,
Bi 'l-mantiqi 'l-badee'i; Abghee bihaa mu'ammalee

Wa saabi'i 'l-wilaadah; Wa maa ataahu 's-saadah,
Li wafqi maa araadah; Ilaahuhu fi 'l-azali,

Tahni'atu 'r-Rabi'i; Bi madhati 'sh-Shafee'i,
Bi 'l-mantiqi 'l-badee'i; Abghee bihaa mu'ammalee

Ahlan bi yawmi summee; Muhammadan khayra 'smi,
Ramzan li ma'na 'l-ismi; Min jaddihi li yanjalee,

Tahni'atu 'r-Rabi'i; Bi madhati 'sh-Shafee'i,
Bi 'l-mantiqi 'l-badee'i; Abghee bihaa mu'ammalee

Bi hamdi 'l-awwaleenaa; Lahu wa 'l-aakhireenaa,
Fa kaana Dhaa yaqeenaa; Mina 'l-Kareemi 'l-Mifdali,

Tahni'atu 'r-Rabi'i; Bi madhati 'sh-Shafee'i,
Bi 'l-mantiqi 'l-badee'i; Abghee bihaa mu'ammalee

Ahlan bi yawmi 'thnayni; Mawlidi thani 'thnayni,
Mab'athi sirri 'l-kawni; Maqdamihi 'l-mubajjali,

Tahni'atu 'r-Rabi'i; Bi madhati 'sh-Shafee'i,
Bi 'l-mantiqi 'l-badee'i; Abghee bihaa mu'ammalee

Ahlan bi sharhi 'l-'ajami; Ibreela shahri 'l-karami,
Akrim bi ardi 'l-harami; Mawlid khayri mursali,

Tahni'atu 'r-Rabi'i; Bi madhati 'sh-Shafee'i,
Bi 'l-mantiqi 'l-badee'i; Abghee bihaa mu'ammalee

Akrim bi yawmin saaraa; 'Ishreena wa 'stanaaraa,
Bi man hawa 'l-fakhaaraa; Wa ghufratin wa min manzili,

Tahni'atu 'r-Rabi'i; Bi madhati 'sh-Shafee'i,
Bi 'l-mantiqi 'l-badee'i; Abghee bihaa mu'ammalee

Akrim bi Shahri 'n-neesaan; Mawlidi Khayri insaan,
Qudwati ahli 'l-ihsaani; Wa Kaamili 'l-mukammali,

Tahni'atu 'r-Rabi'i; Bi madhati 'sh-Shafee'i,
Bi 'l-mantiqi 'l-badee'i; Abghee bihaa mu'ammalee

Qad tammati 'l-la'aalee; Fee 'iddati 'l-layaalee,
Fee zeenati 'l-ma'aalee; Ka jawhari 'l-mufassali,

Tahni'atu 'r-Rabi'i; Bi madhati 'sh-Shafee'i,
Bi 'l-mantiqi 'l-badee'i; Abghee bihaa mu'ammalee

Tahni'atu 'r-rabee'i; Bi madhati 'sh-shafee'i,
Bi 'l-mantiqi 'l-badee'i; Abghee bihaa mu'ammalee,

Tahni'atu 'r-Rabi'i; Bi madhati 'sh-Shafee'i,
Bi 'l-mantiqi 'l-badee'i; Abghee bihaa mu'ammalee

Abghee biha 'l-jam'a bihi; Yawman wa nayla qurbihi,
Wa fadla hubbi Rabbihi; Wa man ridaahu amalee,

Tahni'atu 'r-Rabi'i; Bi madhati 'sh-Shafee'i,
Bi 'l-mantiqi 'l-badee'i; Abghee bihaa mu'ammalee

Wa 'l-khatma lee bi 'l-husnaa; Wa 'l-jam'a lee bi 'l-hasnaa,
Lada 'l-maqaami 'l-asnaa; Ma'a 'r-rafeeqi 'l-afdali,

Tahni'atu 'r-Rabi'i; Bi madhati 'sh-Shafee'i,
Bi 'l-mantiqi 'l-badee'i; Abghee bihaa mu'ammalee

Wa kun lanaa Waliyyan; Wa Naasiran Hafiyyan,
Laa nakhtashee ghawiyyan; Bi jaahi 'abdika 'l-'alee,

Tahni'atu 'r-Rabi'i; Bi madhati 'sh-Shafee'i,
Bi 'l-mantiqi 'l-badee'i; Abghee bihaa mu'ammalee

Sallaa wa sallama 'l-Ilahi; 'Alayhi afdala 's-salaah,
Maa daama kawnuhu ilaah; Min abadin li azali,

Tahni'atu 'r-Rabi'i; Bi madhati 'sh-Shafee'i,
Bi 'l-mantiqi 'l-badee'i; Abghee bihaa mu'ammalee

Wa aalihi wa sahbihi; Wa zawjihi wa hizbihi,
Wa kulli aali hubbihi; Ma'a 's-salaami 'l-akmali

Translation of Poem

We welcome to the (month) of Rabi'; With the praise
of the Intercessor
With beautiful speech; By which I seek to obtain
my hope,

Our Lord! Bless; The best of mankind who elevated,
Above the exalted Heavens; With the permission of his
Exalted Lord,

We welcome to the (month) of Rabi'; With the praise
of the Intercessor
With beautiful speech; By which I seek to obtain
my hope

Welcome to the month of the birth; The month of
exaltedness and mastery,
The month of the Prophet Ahmad; The month of Rabi'
al-Awwal,

We welcome to the (month) of Rabi'; With the praise
of the Intercessor
With beautiful speech; By which I seek to obtain
my hope

He was distinguished with the spring; Because he is like the spring,
To the earth and the intercessor; For every difficult calamity,

We welcome to the (month) of Rabi'; With the praise of the Intercessor
With beautiful speech; By which I seek to obtain my hope

Welcome to the month of felicity; The month of the departure of sorrows,
Our pride and jubilation; The month of the best Prophet,

We welcome to the (month) of Rabi'; With the praise of the Intercessor
With beautiful speech; By which I seek to obtain my hope

The month of happiness and elation; The month that has authority over time,
Which stands out among the months; Being crowned and enthroned,

We welcome to the (month) of Rabi'; With the praise of the Intercessor
With beautiful speech; By which I seek to obtain my hope

Welcome to the month of the Opener; Of the locks of being, the Opener,
Who was distinguished with the openings; And obtained the seal of creeds,

We welcome to the (month) of Rabi'; With the praise of the Intercessor
With beautiful speech; By which I seek to obtain my hope

Welcome to the month of the criterion; The month of the Prophet who distributes,
The Opener and the Seal; The Last and the First,

We welcome to the (month) of Rabi'; With the praise of the Intercessor
With beautiful speech; By which I seek to obtain my hope

Welcome to the month of the helper; Of the Truth, the month of the commander,
To good, the month of the one who appeared; With every perfect attribute,

We welcome to the (month) of Rabi'; With the praise of the Intercessor
With beautiful speech; By which I seek to obtain my hope

Welcome to the month of the Guide; To the path of guidance,
The conductor and guide; To the best path,

We welcome to the (month) of Rabi'; With the praise of the Intercessor
With beautiful speech; By which I seek to obtain my hope

Welcome to the month of the Master; Of whites and of blacks,
Who will enjoy complete mastery; On the day in which the Messengers will excuse themselves,

We welcome to the (month) of Rabi'; With the praise of the Intercessor
With beautiful speech; By which I seek to obtain my hope

And he will have sufficed the affair; Completely, its burdens and its duties,
By his saying, "I am the one to accomplish this"; When its dread will have increased,

We welcome to the (month) of Rabi'; With the praise of the Intercessor
With beautiful speech; By which I seek to obtain my hope

And how much of a relief; Will be the response he receives,
From his Lord, "Ask and you will receive"; And intercede with us, it will be accepted,

We welcome to the (month) of Rabi'; With the praise of the Intercessor
With beautiful speech; By which I seek to obtain my hope

Welcome to the month of the Chosen One; The elect among all God's chosen,
The best of slaves, who was chosen; Among Angels and Messengers,

We welcome to the (month) of Rabi'; With the praise of the Intercessor
With beautiful speech; By which I seek to obtain my hope

The month of the Best of creation; The month of he of beautiful character,

The month of the possessor of great character; As mentioned in the clear revelation,

We welcome to the (month) of Rabi'; With the praise of the Intercessor
With beautiful speech; By which I seek to obtain my hope

The month of he whose God; Preferred him and chose him,
Whose love [God] preferred; When He decreed all things,

We welcome to the (month) of Rabi'; With the praise of the Intercessor
With beautiful speech; By which I seek to obtain my hope

The month of he who had not done evil; Who had only done the best things,
To him Jibril descended; In complete light he ascended,

We welcome to the (month) of Rabi'; With the praise of the Intercessor
With beautiful speech; By which I seek to obtain my hope

Welcome to the twelfth night; In it and its luminous day,
The perfume of that morning; And the light of the emergence of its horizon,

We welcome to the (month) of Rabi'; With the praise of the Intercessor
With beautiful speech; By which I seek to obtain my hope

Welcome to everything that manifest; Of miracles and things which the intellect cannot bear,
Such as his raising his sight; Towards his elevated station,

We welcome to the (month) of Rabi'; With the praise of the Intercessor
With beautiful speech; By which I seek to obtain my hope

And what wonders Aminah; Saw when he raised his,
Index finger and then drew near; With a humble prostration,

We welcome to the (month) of Rabi'; With the praise of the Intercessor
With beautiful speech; By which I seek to obtain my hope

Likewise, the descent of radiance; Also, the castles being shown,
In it and the falling; And breaking of the idols,

We welcome to the (month) of Rabi'; With the praise of the Intercessor
With beautiful speech; By which I seek to obtain my hope

The sea level was lowered; The rivers dried up,
Because of him and the fire; Was put out because of shame,

We welcome to the (month) of Rabi'; With the praise of the Intercessor
With beautiful speech; By which I seek to obtain my hope

And their jinn became disappointed; From stars being cast at them,
And from being expelled from where they sat; On account of the Best of Messengers,

We welcome to the (month) of Rabi'; With the praise of the Intercessor
With beautiful speech; By which I seek to obtain my hope

The Shaytan shrieked; On account of the greatness of his affair,
One of the clearest proofs; For the immensity of the affliction he was caused,

We welcome to the (month) of Rabi'; With the praise of the Intercessor
With beautiful speech; By which I seek to obtain my hope

The Possessor of Generosity blessed us; With the best of men,
In the best of nights; In the best of lands,

We welcome to the (month) of Rabi'; With the praise of the Intercessor
With beautiful speech; By which I seek to obtain my hope

Welcome to a day of Eid; Which no Eid can equal,
In which the noble birth has taken place; In the mansion of Saturn[6],

---

[6] A reference to the place of Saturn in the sky at the time of the birth

We welcome to the (month) of Rabi'; With the praise of the Intercessor
With beautiful speech; By which I seek to obtain my hope

And the seventh day after the birth; And the nobility that came to it,
Corresponding to that which his God; Had willed in sempiternity,

We welcome to the (month) of Rabi'; With the praise of the Intercessor
With beautiful speech; By which I seek to obtain my hope

Welcome to the day he was named; Muhammad, the best of names,
An allusion to the name's meaning; by his grandfather, that he may obtain,

We welcome to the (month) of Rabi'; With the praise of the Intercessor
With beautiful speech; By which I seek to obtain my hope

The praise for him; Of the first and the last of us,
And that certainly came to pass; Through the Grace of the all-Generous,

We welcome to the (month) of Rabi'; With the praise of the Intercessor
With beautiful speech; By which I seek to obtain my hope

Welcome to the twelfth day; The birth of the second being,

The repository of the secret of creation; Its honored forerunner,

We welcome to the (month) of Rabi'; With the praise of the Intercessor
With beautiful speech; By which I seek to obtain my hope

Welcome to the non-Arab month; Of April[7], the month of generosity,
Bless the earth of the Sanctuary; The birthplace of the best of Messengers,

We welcome to the (month) of Rabi'; With the praise of the Intercessor
With beautiful speech; By which I seek to obtain my hope

Blessed is the day of the; Twentieth, illuminated,
By the one who obtained nobility; And the stage of the moon called Ghufrah,

We welcome to the (month) of Rabi'; With the praise of the Intercessor
With beautiful speech; By which I seek to obtain my hope

Bless the month of Neesan[8]; The birth of the best of mankind,
The exemplar of the people of excellence; And the perfect and accomplished one,

We welcome to the (month) of Rabi'; With the praise of the Intercessor

---

7   April is the Roman month in which the Prophet ﷺ was born
8   Neesan is the Persian name of the month

With beautiful speech; By which I seek to obtain my hope

These precious verses are completed; In a number of nights,
In ascendant beauty; Like a distinguished ruby,

We welcome to the (month) of Rabi'; With the praise of the Intercessor
With beautiful speech; By which I seek to obtain my hope

Greetings to Rabi'; With the praise of the intercessor,
With beautified speech; By which I seek to obtain my hopes,

We welcome to the (month) of Rabi'; With the praise of the Intercessor
With beautiful speech; By which I seek to obtain my hope

I seek through it to be gathered with him; One day and win his nearness,
And the graceful love of his Lord; The One whose satisfaction is my goal,

We welcome to the (month) of Rabi'; With the praise of the Intercessor
With beautiful speech; By which I seek to obtain my hope

And that He concludes my life in goodness; And gather me in the place of goodness,
In the highest of stations; With the best of neighbors,

We welcome to the (month) of Rabi'; With the praise of the Intercessor
With beautiful speech; By which I seek to obtain my hope

And be for us a Protector; And a hidden Helper,
That we may not fear any temptation; By the status of Your exalted slave,

We welcome to the (month) of Rabi'; With the praise of the Intercessor
With beautiful speech; By which I seek to obtain my hope

May God send blessings and peace; With the best of blessings,
That lasts as long as He is God; From eternity to sempiternity,

We welcome to the (month) of Rabi'; With the praise of the Intercessor
With beautiful speech; By which I seek to obtain my hope

And his family and companions; His wife and his party,
And the family of all his lovers; Along with the most perfect greeting of peace

We welcome to the (month) of Rabi'; With the praise of the Intercessor
With beautiful speech; By which I seek to obtain my hope

بِجَاهِهِمْ يَاإِلَهِي اغْفِرْ لِنَاظِمِهَا
وَاسْمَحْ لِقَارِئِهَا وَلِلَّذِي حَضَرَهْ

وَعُمَّهُمْ بِخَفِيِّ الْلُطْفِ وَاكْفِهِمْ
نَوَائِبَ الدَّهْرِ مَعْ ءَآفَاتِهِ الْكَدِرَهْ

أَجِبْ دُعَاهُمْ وَعَجِّلْ بِالَّذِي طَلَبُواْ
بِجَاهِ أَحْمد مع أصحابه الخيره

Bi jaahihim yaa Ilaahi 'ghfir li naazimihaa,
Wa 'smah li qaari'ihaa wa li 'lladhee hadarahu,

Wa 'ummahum bi khafiyyi 'l-lutfi wa 'kfihim,
Nawaa'iba 'd-dahra ma'a aafaatihi 'l-kadirih,

Ajib da'aahum wa 'ajjil bi 'lladhee taboo,
Bi jaahi Ahmada ma' ashaabihi 'l-khiyarah

By their status, o, my God! Forgive the composer (of this poem),
And pardon its reciter and all those who are present,

Cover them in a hidden gentle mercy and suffice them,
The misfortunes of life and it's difficult trials,

Answer their supplication and hasten that which they seek,
By the status of Ahmad along with his elect companions

اَللَّهُمَّ صَلِّ عَلَى سَيِّدِنَا مُحَمَّدٍ الفَاتِحِ لِمَا أُغْلِقَ وَالخَاتِمِ لِمَا سَبَقَ نَاصِرِ الحَقِّ بِالحَقِّ وَالهَادِي إِلَى صِرَاطِكَ المُسْتَقِيمِ وَعَلَى آلِهِ حَقَّ قَدْرِهِ وَمِقْدَارِهِ العَظِيمِ، صَلَاةً تَفْتَحُ لَنَا بِهَا أَبْوَابَ الرِّضَى وَالتَّيْسِيرِ، وَتُغْلِقُ بِنَا عَنَّا أَبْوَابَ الشَّرِّ وَالتَّعْسِيرِ، وَتَكُونُ لَنَا بِهَا وَلِيًّا نَصِيرًا، أَنْتَ مَوْلَانَا فَنِعْمَ المَوْلَى وَنِعْمَ النَّصِيرُ، سُبْحَانَ رَبِّكَ رَبِّ العِزَّةِ عَمَّا يَصِفُونَ وَسَلَامٌ عَلَى المُرْسَلِينَ وَالحَمْدُ لِلَّهِ رَبِّ العَالَمِينَ

Allahumma salli 'alaa Sayyidinaa Muhammadin al-Faatihi li maa ughliqa wal Khaatimi li maa sabaqa Naasiril haqqi bil haqqi wal Haadee ilaa siraatikal mustaqeemi wa 'alaa aalihi haqqa qadrihi wa miqdaarihil 'azeemi. Salaatan taftahu lanaa bihaa abwaabar ridaa wat tayseeri wa tughliqu bihaa 'annaa abwaabash sharri wat ta'seeri wa takoonu lanaa bihaa Waliyyan wa Naseeran Anta Waliyyunaa wa Mawlaanaa fa ni'aml Mawlaa wa ni'man Naseer. Subhaana Rabbika Rabbil 'izzati 'ammaa yasifoona wa salaamun 'alal Mursaleena wal hamdu li Llahi Rabbil 'aalameen

O, Allah! Bless our Master Muhammad, the Opener of that which was closed; the Seal of what went before; the Helper of the Truth by the Truth; and the Guide to Your Straight Path, and his family in accordance with his grandeur and immense worth. Let it be a blessing that opens for us the doors of Your satisfaction and facilitation; closes the door to evil and difficulty; and by which You will be a Protector and a Helper. You are our Protector and our Lord. And how excellent a Lord. How excellent a Helper. Blessed be Your Lord, the Lord of Might, above that which they attributed [to Him]. Peace to be upon the Messengers. And all praise is due to Allah, Lord of the worlds.

www.ingramcontent.com/pod-product-compliance
Lightning Source LLC
Chambersburg PA
CBHW061224070526
44584CB00029B/3971